Square

Square is a plane figure with four equal straigh right angles.

- A square has 4 sides and 4 corners.
- All the sides of a square are equal in length.
- All interior angles are equal and right angles(The sum of the all the interior angles is 360°).

A right angle(90°) is represented by the symbol ∟.

same sign means having equal length

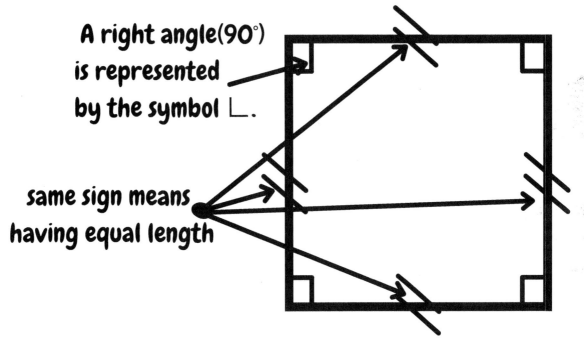

Square in our life:

Chess Board

Square Clock

Let's do it!
Complete the square:

trace a square

How many square in this shape?

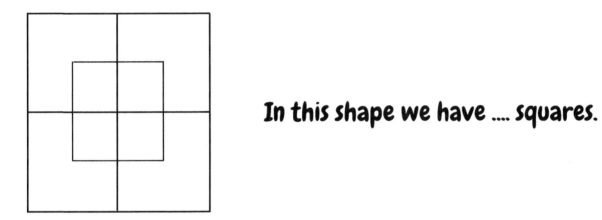

In this shape we have 5 squares.

WORK TIME

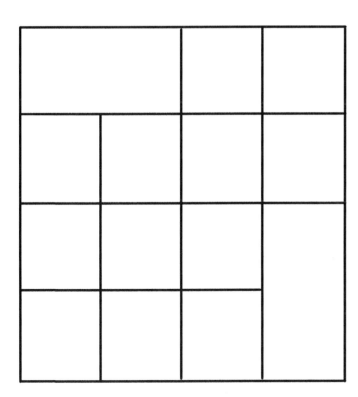

In this shape we have .... squares.

In this shape we have .... squares.

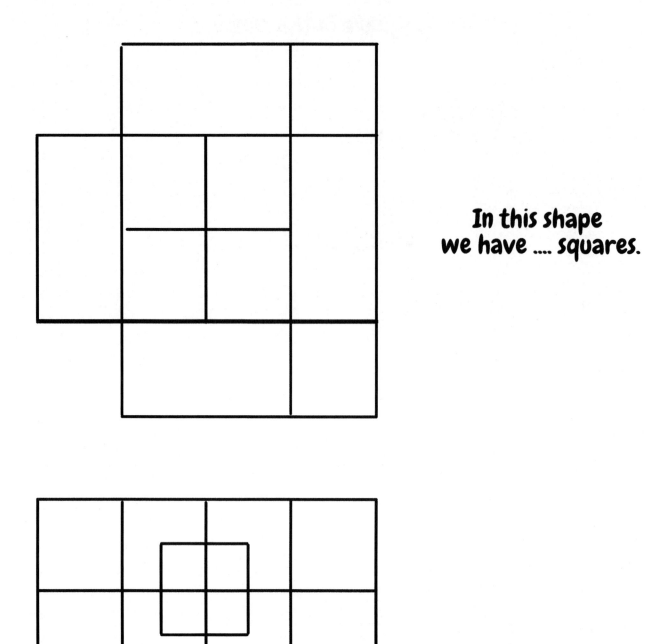

In this shape we have .... squares.

In this shape we have .... squares.

square area and perimeter.

If 'a' denotes the side of the square, then, length of each side of a square is 'a'.

Perimeter of square = AB+BC+CD+DA
$$= a + a + a + a$$
$$= 4a$$

Perimeter of the square = 4a

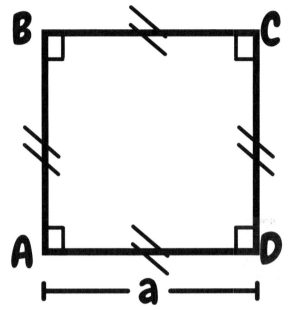

Area = side × side
$$= a \times a$$
$$= a^2$$

Area of the square = a × a = a^2

1. Find the perimeter and area of a square of side 10 cm.

Perimeter of the square :
_____
_____
_____
_____

Area of the square :
_____
_____
_____

WORK TIME

1. Find the perimeter and area of the four little squares and the big square.

The little squares

Perimeter :
_____
_____
_____
_____

Area :
_____
_____
_____

The big square

Perimeter :
_____
_____
_____

Area :
_____
_____
_____

WORK TIME

1. Find the perimeter and area of the four little squares and the big square. if $a = 2b$ and $b = 3$cm.

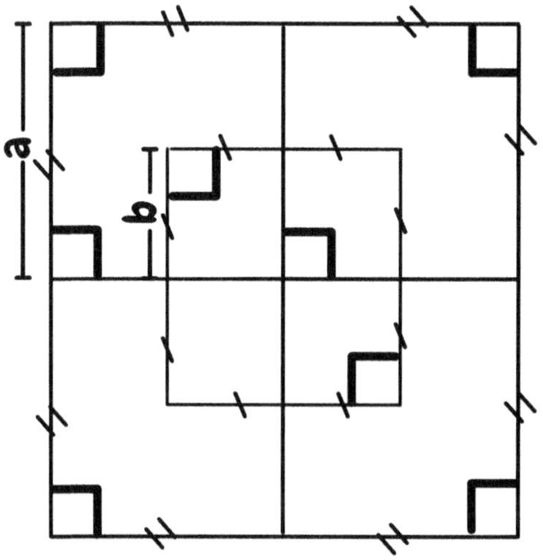

The center squares

Perimeter:

Area:

The big square

Perimeter:

Area:

Answers

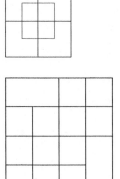

In this shape we have 10 squares.

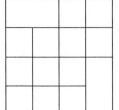

In this shape we have 23 squares.

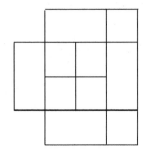

In this shape we have 11 squares.

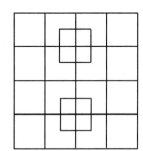

In this shape we have 40 squares.

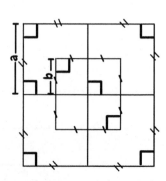

|— 10 cm —|

perimeter=40cm

area= 100cm²

little one:
perimeter=16cm
area= 16cm²
big one:
perimeter=32cm
area= 64 cm²

little one:
perimeter=24cm
area= 36cm²
big one:
perimeter=96cm
area= 144 cm²

Circle

A circle is a round shaped figure that has no corners or edges.

The center of a circle is the center point in a circle from which all the distances to the points on the circle are equal.

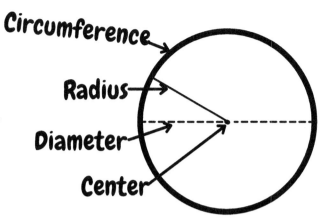

The distance between any point of the circle and the center is called the radius.

Circumference: the length of one circuit along the circle, or the distance around the circle.

Diameter: a line segment whose endpoints lie on the circle and that passes through the center.(<u>Diameter = 2 x radius</u>.)

Circle in our life:

Mirror

Coins

Let's do it!
Complete the Circle:

trace a circle

Work Time

Choose all answers that apply:

Which of the segments in the circle below is a radius?

- A
- B
- C
- D

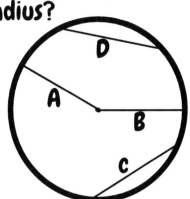

Which of the segments in the circle below is a diameter?

- A
- B
- C

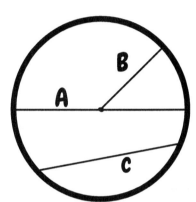

Find the diameter of the circle shown below.

The diameter: ....

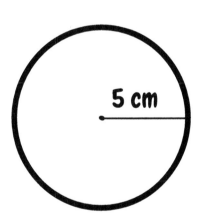

Find the radius of the circle shown below.

The radius: ....

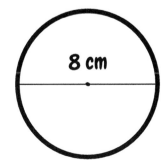

Circumference of a circle

In geometry, the circumference is the perimeter of a circle. That is, the circumference would be the arc length of the circle, as if it were opened up and straightened out to a line segment. More generally, the perimeter is the curve length around any closed figure.

$$C = 2\pi r = \pi d$$

C: circumference.

r: radius.

d: diameter

π: is a mathematical constant ($\pi = 3,14\ldots\ldots$).

Example:

$C = 2\pi r$
　$= 2 \times \pi \times 2$
　$= 4\pi$ cm.

We can just leave our answer like that in terms of π.

Or, we can calculate with the approximate value of $\pi = 3.14$.

$C = 2\pi r$
　$= 2 \times 3.14 \times 2$
　$= 12.56$ cm.

Circumference of a circle

Find the circumference of the circle shown below.

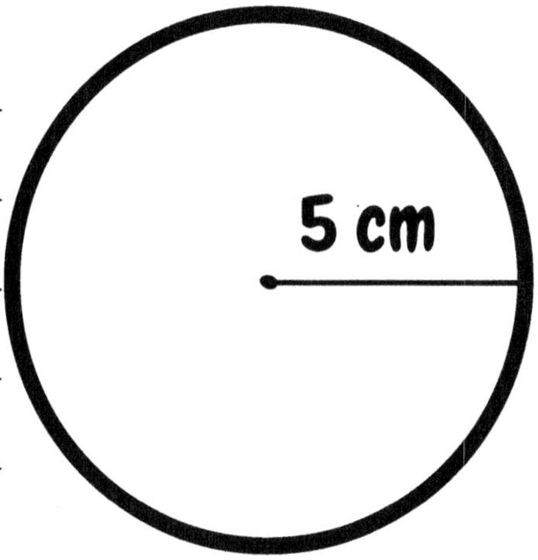

------

5 cm

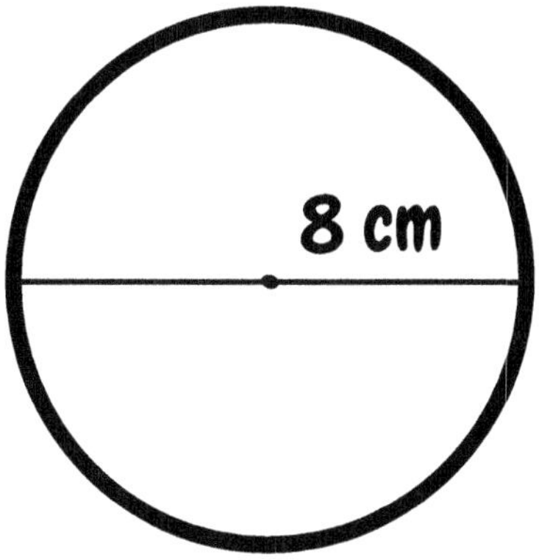

8 cm

Find the arc length of the semicircle.

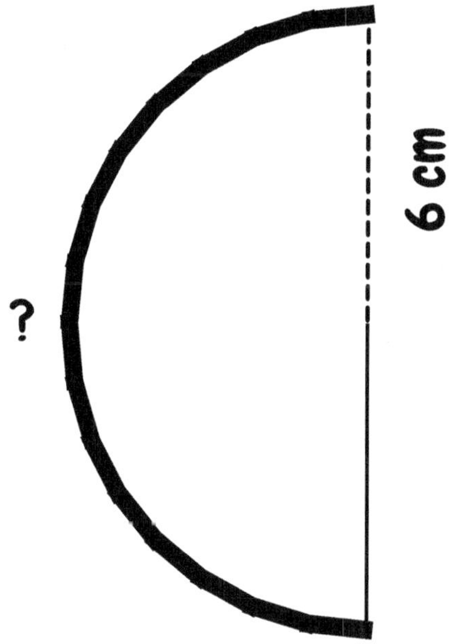

6 cm

?

Area of a circle

Area = A = π r r = π r²

In geometry, the area enclosed by a circle of radius r is πr².

Example:

$A = \pi (3)^2 = 9\pi$ unites².

or,

$A = \pi (3)^2 = 28.26$ cm².

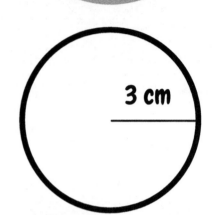

Relating circumference and area

We have: $C = 2\pi r$ and $A = \pi r^2$

we divide both sides of the circumference by 2π: $\dfrac{C}{2\pi} = \dfrac{2\pi r}{2\pi}$

$r = \dfrac{C}{2\pi}$

we include this relation in the area:

$A = \pi \left(\dfrac{C}{2\pi}\right)^2 = \dfrac{C^2}{4\pi}$

$$A = \dfrac{C^2}{4\pi}$$

A circle has a circumference of 28.26 cm.
What is the diameter of the circle?

Find the area of a circle with a radius of 3.

Find the area of a circle with a diameter of 6.

Find the area of a circle with a circumference of 12.56 cm.

Find the arc length of the partial circle.

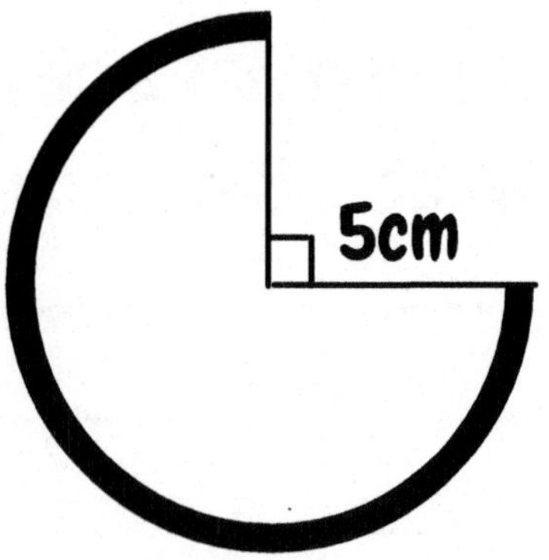

_____
_____
_____
_____
_____

5cm

Find the arc length of the semicircle.

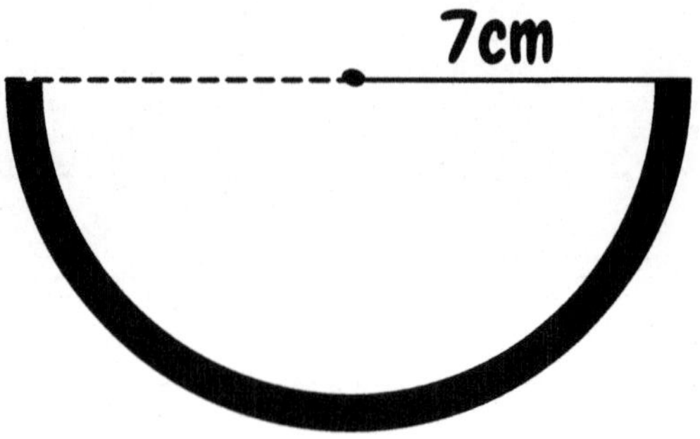

_____
_____
_____
_____
_____

7cm

Find the area of the semicircle.

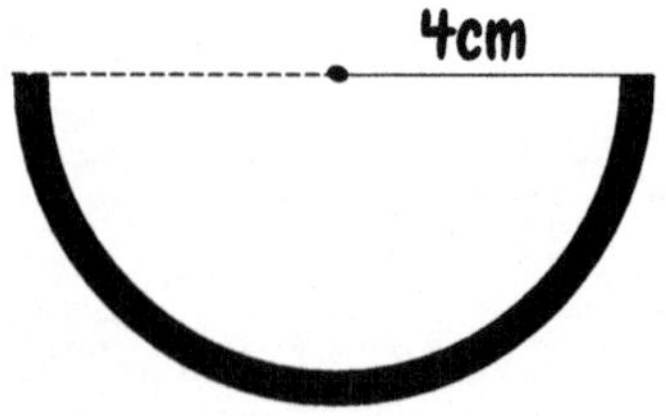

_____
_____
_____
_____
_____

4cm

Find the area of the shape.

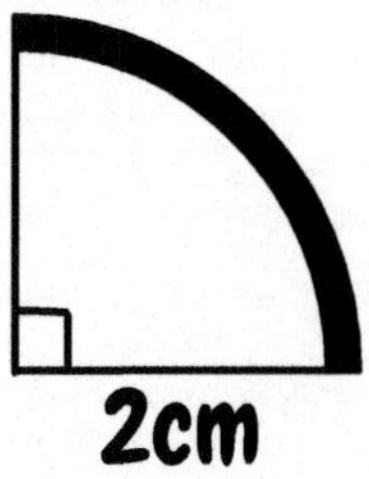

_____
_____
_____
_____
_____

2cm

Answers

Which of the segments in the circle below is a radius?

- B

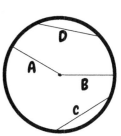

Which of the segments in the circle below is a diameter?

- A

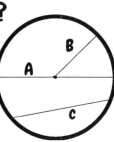

Find the diameter of the circle shown below.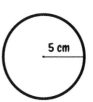
The diameter: 10cm

Find the radius of the circle shown below.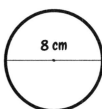
The radius: 4cm

Find the circumference of the circle shown below.

$C = 2 \times 3.14 \times 5 = 31.4$ cm

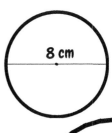

$C = 2 \times 3.14 \times 4 = 25.12$ cm

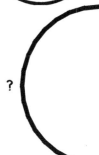

Find the arc length of the semicircle.

$C = 2 \times 3.14 \times 3 = 18.84$cm

the length of the arc = $C/2$ = 9.42 cm

A circle has a circumference of 28.26 cm.
What is the diameter of the circle?
$$r = c/2\pi$$
$$r = 28.26 / 2 \times 3.14 = 4.5 \text{ cm}$$

Find the area of a circle with a radius of 3.
$$a = \pi r^2 = 3.14 \times (3)^2 = 28.26 \text{ cm}^2$$

Find the area of a circle with a diameter of 6.
$$a = \pi (d/2)^2 = 3.14 \times (6/2)^2 = 28.26 \text{ cm}^2$$

Find the area of a circle with a circumference of 12.56 cm.
$$a = C^2 / 4\pi = (12.56)^2 / 4 \times 3.14 = 12.56 \text{ cm}^2$$

Find the arc length of the partial circle.
$$C = 2\pi r = 2 \times 3.14 \times 5 = 31.4 \text{ cm}$$
$$arc = C * 3/4 = 23.55 \text{ cm}$$

Find the arc length of the semicircle.
$$C = 2\pi r = 2 \times 3.14 \times 7 = 43.96 \text{ cm}$$
$$arc = C * 2 = 21.98 \text{ cm}$$

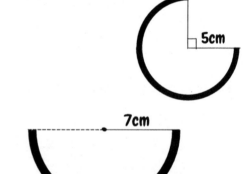

Find the area of the semicircle:
$$a = \pi r^2 = 3.14 \times 4^2 = 50.24 \text{ cm}^2$$
semicircle area $= a/2 = 25.12 \text{ cm}^2$

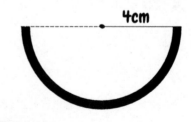

Find the area of the shape:
$$a = \pi r^2 = 3.14 \times 2^2 = 12.56 \text{ cm}^2$$
semicircle area $= a/4 = 3.14 \text{ cm}^2$

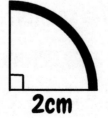

Triangle

A triangle is a polygon with three edges and three vertices. It is one of the basic shapes in geometry. A triangle with vertices A, B, and C is denoted \triangle ABC.

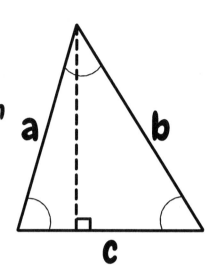

In Euclidean geometry, any three points, when non-collinear, determine a unique triangle

Properties of a Triangle:

- A triangle has three sides, three vertices, and three angles.

roadside signboard

- The sum of the three interior angles of a triangle is always 180°.

- The sum of the length of two sides of a triangle is always greater than the length of the third side.

Types of triangle:

Triangles can be classified according to the lengths of their sides:

- An equilateral triangle has three sides of the same length. An equilateral triangle is also a regular polygon with all angles measuring 60°.
- An isosceles triangle has two sides of equal length. An isosceles triangle also has two angles of the same measure, namely the angles opposite to the two sides of the same length.
- A scalene triangle has all its sides of different lengths. Equivalently, it has all angles of different measure.

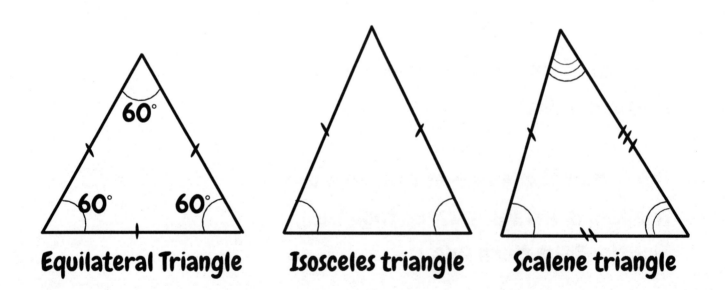

Equilateral Triangle   Isosceles triangle   Scalene triangle

Types of triangle:
By internal angles:

A <u>right triangle</u> has one of its interior angles measuring 90° (a right angle).
The side opposite to the right angle is the hypotenuse, the longest side of the triangle.

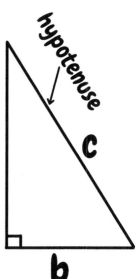

- Right triangles obey the Pythagorean theorem: the sum of the squares of the lengths of the two legs is equal to the square of the length of the hypotenuse: $a^2 + b^2 = c^2$.

   (where a and b are the lengths of the legs and c is the length of the hypotenuse.)

Triangles that do not have an angle measuring 90° are called <u>oblique triangles.</u>

A triangle with all interior angles measuring less than 90° is an <u>acute triangle</u>.

A triangle with one interior angle measuring more than 90° is an <u>obtuse triangle</u>.

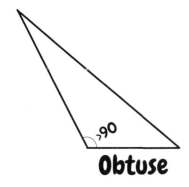
Obtuse

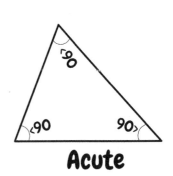
Acute

Area and Perimeter of triangle

The perimeter of a triangle is the sum of the length of its three sides.

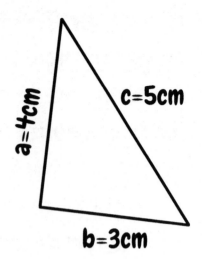

Example:

perimeter = a + b + c = 4 + 3 + 5 = 12 cm.

The area of a triangle is equal to the basis multiplied by the height divided by 2.
When we know the base and height it is easy.

$$\text{Area} = \frac{\text{high} \times \text{base}}{2}$$

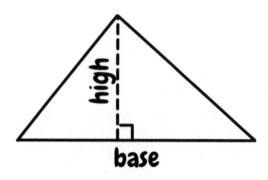

The most important thing is that the base and height are at right angles.

1-Area of a Right Angled Triangle:

Area of a Right Triangle = ½ × Base × Height (Perpendicular distance)
= 1/2 × AB × AC
= 1/2 a b

example:
Area = 1/2 × base × height
= 1/2 MH × ME
= 1/2 × 3 × 4 = 6 cm².

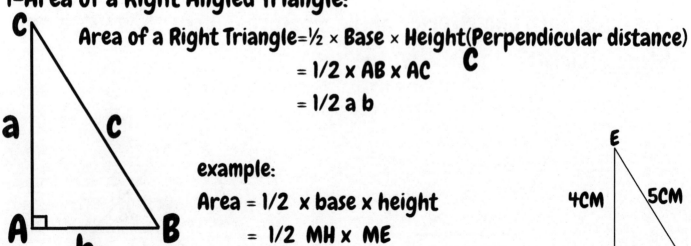

2-Area of an Equilateral Triangle:

Area of an Equilateral Triangle = $A = (\sqrt{3})/4 \times side^2$

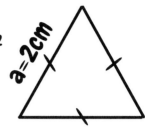

in this example: Area = $(\sqrt{3})/4 \times a^2 = (\sqrt{3})/4 \times 2^2$
= 1.73 cm²

Trigonometric functions

In mathematics, the trigonometric functions are real functions which <u>relate an angle of a right-angled triangle</u> to ratios of two side lengths. They are widely used in all sciences.

The trigonometric functions most widely used in modern mathematics are the sine, the cosine, and the tangent.

Given an acute angle $A = \theta$ of a right-angled triangle, the hypotenuse h is the side that connects the two acute angles. The side b adjacent to θ is the side of the triangle that connects θ to the right angle. The third side a is said to be opposite to θ.

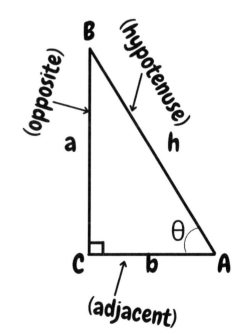

If the angle θ is given, then all sides of the right-angled triangle are well-defined up to a scaling factor.

This means that the ratio of any two side lengths depends only on θ. Thus these three ratios define three functions of θ, which are the trigonometric functions. More precisely, the three trigonometric functions are:

sine:
$$\sin \theta = \frac{a}{h} = \frac{opposite}{hypotenuse}$$

cosine:
$$\cos \theta = \frac{b}{h} = \frac{adjacent}{hypotenuse}$$

tangent:
$$\tan \theta = \frac{a}{b} = \frac{opposite}{adjacent}$$

Example:
the length of side x in the diagram below:

The angle is 60 degrees. We are given the hypotenuse and need to find the adjacent side.

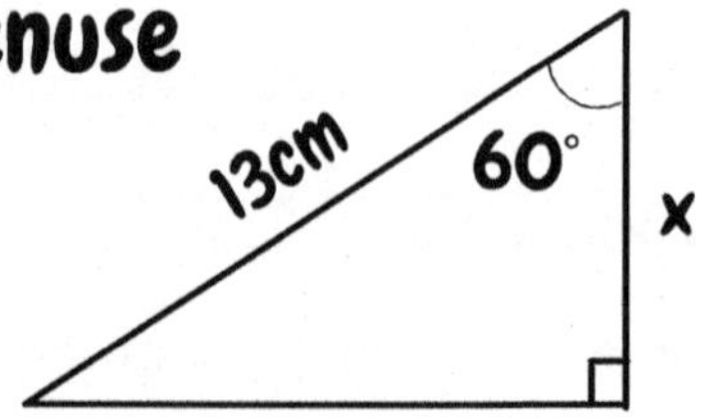

This formula which connects these three is:
cos(θ) = adjacent / hypotenuse

therefore,   cos60 = x / 13
therefore,   x = 13 × cos60 = 6.5cm

the length of side x is 6.5cm.

Example: What is the sine of 35°?

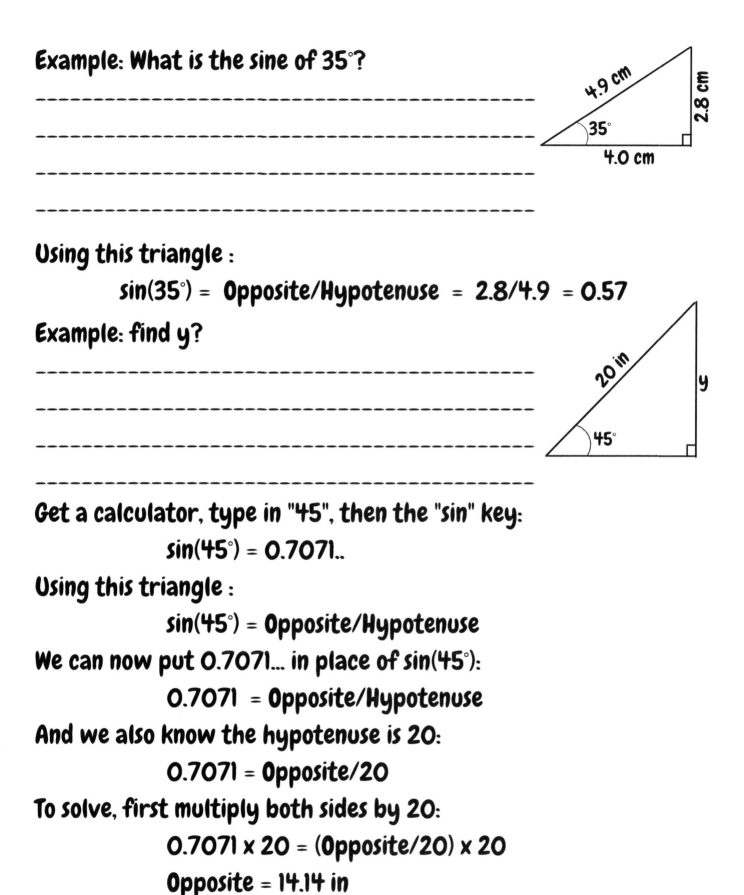

Using this triangle :

$\sin(35°) = $ Opposite/Hypotenuse $= 2.8/4.9 = 0.57$

Example: find y?

Get a calculator, type in "45", then the "sin" key:

$\sin(45°) = 0.7071..$

Using this triangle :

$\sin(45°) = $ Opposite/Hypotenuse

We can now put 0.7071... in place of sin(45°):

$0.7071 = $ Opposite/Hypotenuse

And we also know the hypotenuse is 20:

$0.7071 = $ Opposite/20

To solve, first multiply both sides by 20:

$0.7071 \times 20 = $ (Opposite/20) $\times 20$

Opposite $= 14.14$ in

$y = 14.14$ in

Work Time

W1– Find the area of an acute triangle with a base of 13 inches and a height of 5 inches.

W2– Find the area of a right-angled triangle with a base of 7 cm and a height of 8 cm.

W3– Find the area of an obtuse-angled triangle with a base of 4 cm and a height 7 cm.

W1= $A = (½) \times (13 \text{ in}) \times (5 \text{ in}) = A = 32.5 \text{ in}^2$

W2= $(½) \times (7 \text{ cm}) \times (8 \text{ cm}) = A = 28 \text{ cm}^2$

w3= $(½) \times (4 \text{ cm}) \times (7 \text{ cm}) = A = 14 \text{ cm}^2$

W4 - What is the area of this triangle?

Sides: 10 in, 7 in; included angle: 25°

$$A = \frac{1}{2}(10)(7)\sin(25°)$$
$$A \approx 14.79 \text{ in}^2$$

W5 - What is the area of this triangle?

Sides: 75 m, 150 m; included angle: 123°

$$A = \frac{1}{2}(75)(150)\sin(123°)$$
$$A \approx 4717.24 \text{ m}^2$$

solution of w4:

First of all we must decide what we know:
We know angle C = 25°, and sides b = 10 and a = 7.
So let's get going:
a is the base =10 in so we need the height

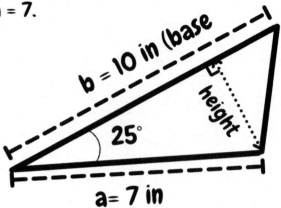

we have, sin (25) = height / a
===> height = a x sin (25)

Area = (1/2) base height
= (1/2) b a x sin (25)
=(1/2) x 10 x 7 x 0.42
= 14.8 in²

solution of w5:

First of all we must decide what we know:
- c = 75 m,
- a = 150 m,
- and angle B = 123°

So let's get going:
c is the base =75 in so we need the height

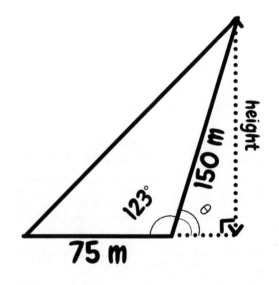

we have, sin (θ) = height / a
===> height = a x sin (θ)
and θ = 180 −123= 57 °

Area = (1/2) base height
= (1/2) c a x sin (57)
=(1/2) x 75 x 150 x 0.84
= 4717 m²

3 Dimensional

Geometry can be divided into two types: plane and solid geometry. Plane geometry deals with flat shapes like square, circle, triangles, lines, etc.,

On the other hand, solid geometry involves objects of three-dimensional shapes such as cubes, spheres, pyramids etc.

three-dimensional shape can be defined as a solid figure or an object or shape that has three dimensions – length, width and height.

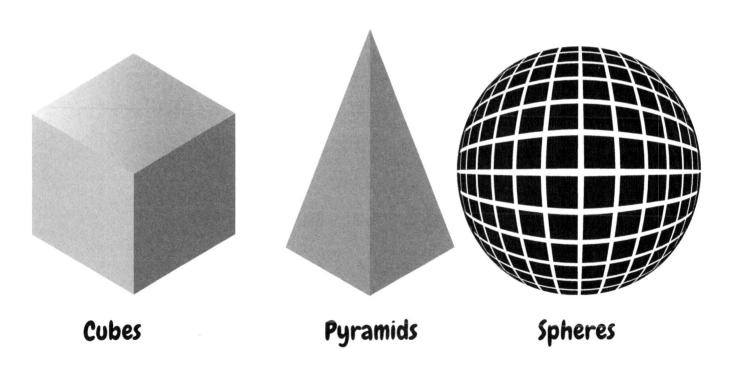

Cubes   Pyramids   Spheres

Cubes

A cube is one of the simplest shapes in three-dimensional space.
All the six faces of a cube are squares, it is a solid or three-dimensional shape which has 6 square faces.

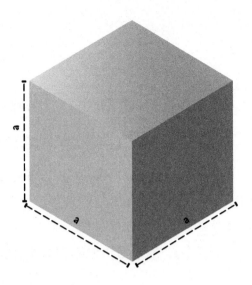

Properties:

- A cube has 6 square faces.
- A cube has 8 points (vertices).
- A cube has 12 edges.
- A square is in many ways like a cube, only in two dimensions rather than three.

Surface Area of a Cube:

Since a cube has six faces, therefore, we need to calculate the surface area of the cube, covered by each face.

Area of one face = Area of a square = a^2.

We know that the cube has 6 square shaped faces.

Total surface area = 6 x Area of one face = $6a^2$.

The volume of a Cube:

can be found with the following formula:

$$Volume = a^3$$

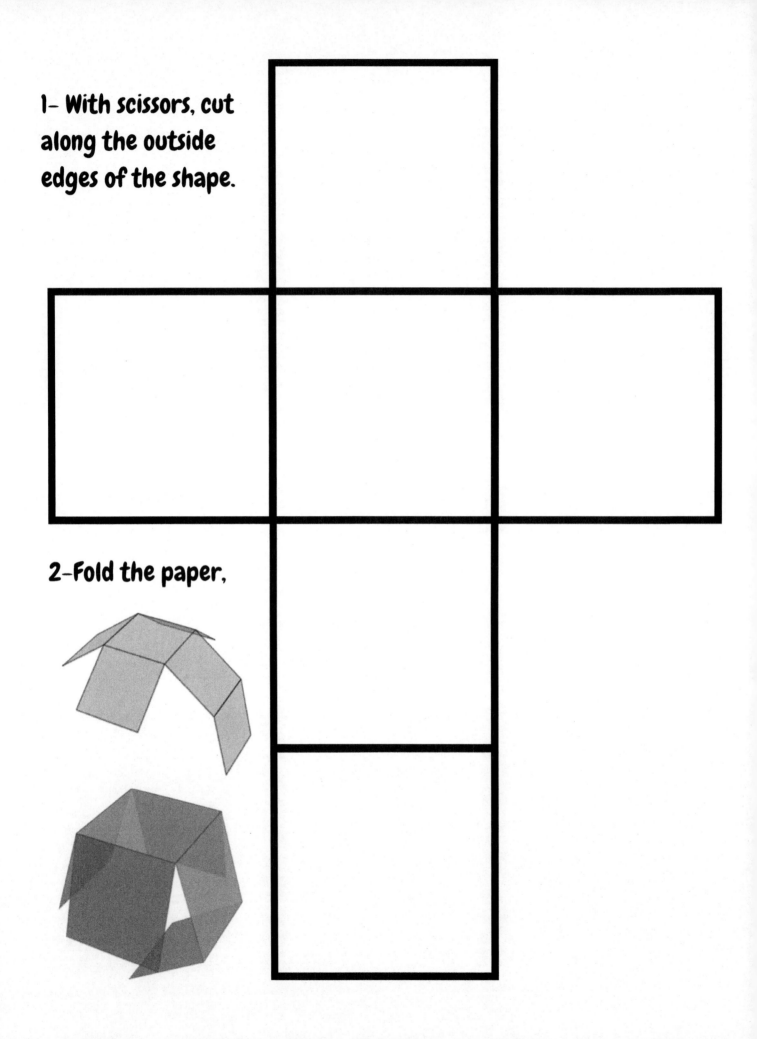

Cube Examples:

Example 1:
If the length of the side of the cube is 10 cm, then find its surface area and volume.

Example 2:
Find the side length of a cube whose volume is 512 cm3.

Example 3:
Find the volume of the cube whose surface area is 24 cm2.

Example 4:

Find the volume of grey cube.

(Note: the blue cube is in the interior of the grey one)

----

14 cm

5 cm

Solution:

Example 1: Surface = 6×10^2 = 600cm².

volume = 10^3 =1000 cm3 (cubic centimeter)

Example 2: side length= $(512)^{(1/3)}$ = 8 cm.

Example 3: surface = $6a^2$ = 24cm²

$a = \sqrt{(24/6)}$ = 2cm

volume= a^3 = 8cm3 (cubic centimeter)

Example 4: volume of blue cube = 5^3 = 125 cm3 (cubic centimeter)

volume of the grey + blue = 14^3 = 2744 cm3 (cubic centimeter)

Volume of grey cube= 2744 – 125 = 2619 cm3 (cubic centimeter).

Pyramid

A pyramid is a structure whose outer surfaces are triangular and converge to a single step at the top (the apex).

The base of a pyramid can be trilateral, quadrilateral, or of any polygon shape.

a pyramid has at least three outer triangular surfaces (at least four faces including the base).

The square pyramid, with a square base and four triangular outer surfaces, is a common version.

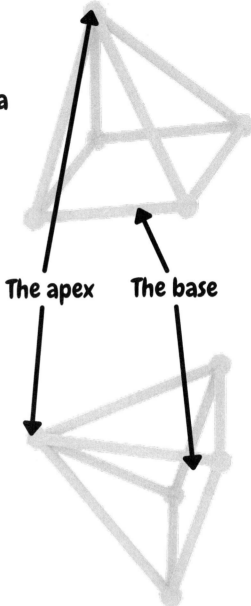

The apex   The base

square pyramid

Pyramid with others polygon base:

Cut and make:

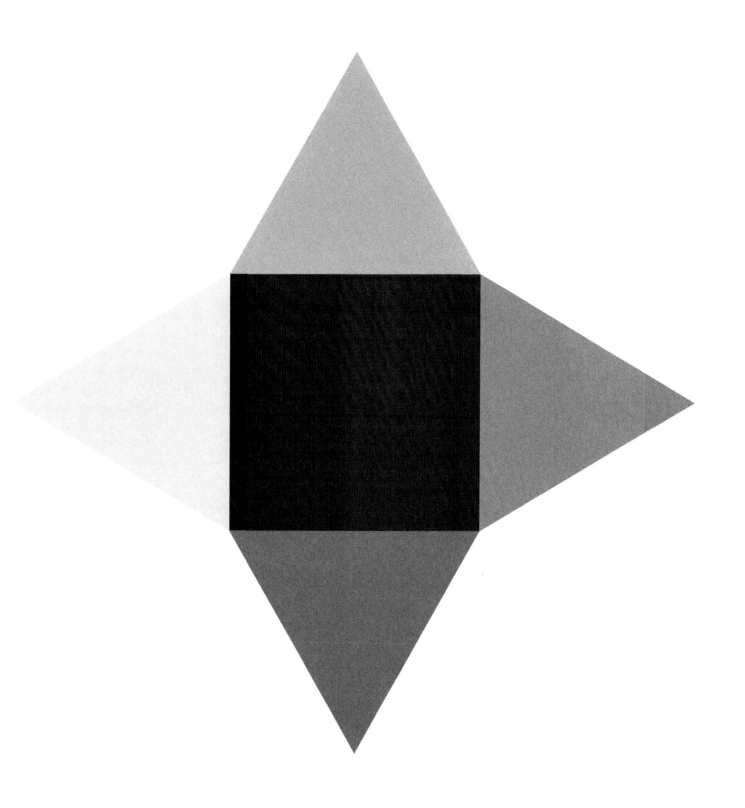

surface area of pyramid

Method 1:

Surface area = A + 1/2 PS

A : Area of base.

P : perimeter of base.

S : slant height.

Method 2:

A = Lw + L($\sqrt{(w/2)^2 + h^2}$) + w($\sqrt{(L/2)^2 + h^2}$)

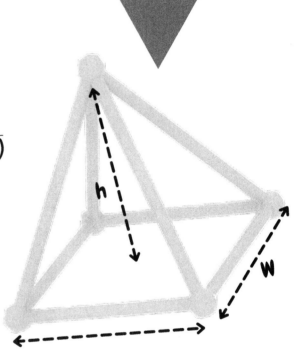

volume of pyramid

volume of pyramid = (a h) / 3

a : base surface.

h pyramid height.

Example:
calculate for each pyramid the surface area and volume:

Results: surface area 1 = surface area 2 = 75 in²

Volume 1 = volume 2 = 36.08 in^3

Spheres

A sphere is a geometrical object in three-dimensional space that is the surface of a ball.

Like a circle in a two-dimensional space, a sphere is defined mathematically as the set of points that are all at the same distance r from a given point in a three-dimensional space.

Volume : $V = (4/3) \pi r^3$

Surface area : $S = 4 \pi r^2$

Examples :

Basketball ball

The moon appears round, and it's natural to assume that it is actually spherical in shape.

Example:
Calculate the surface and the volume :

----

radius = 3in

Calculate the surface and the volume of the semi sphere :

----

radius = 4in

the 1st shape:
surface area : 113.1 in ^ 2
volume : 113.1 in ^ 3
the 2nd one :
surface area : 100.53 in ^ 2
volume : 134.04 in ^ 3

Math Quiz

Example:

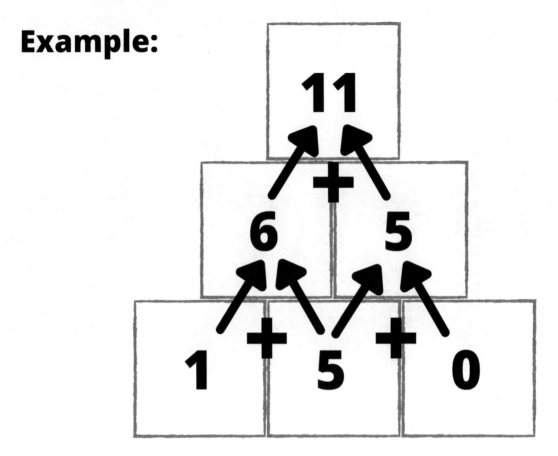

Do:

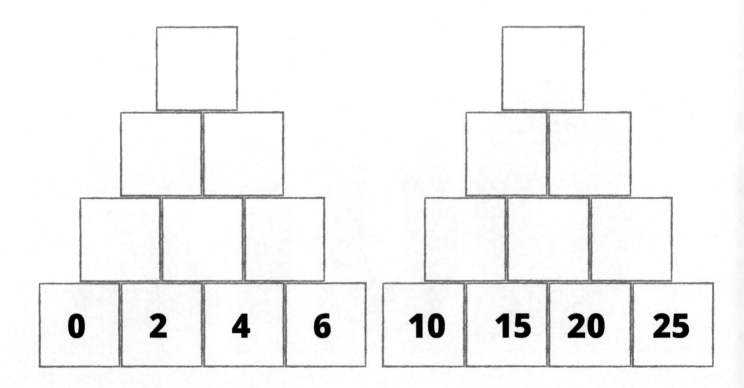

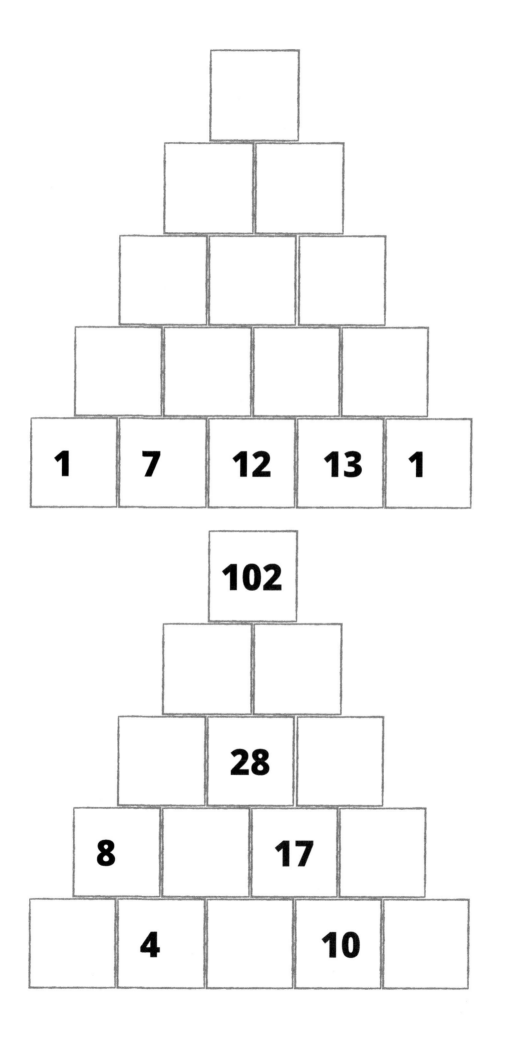

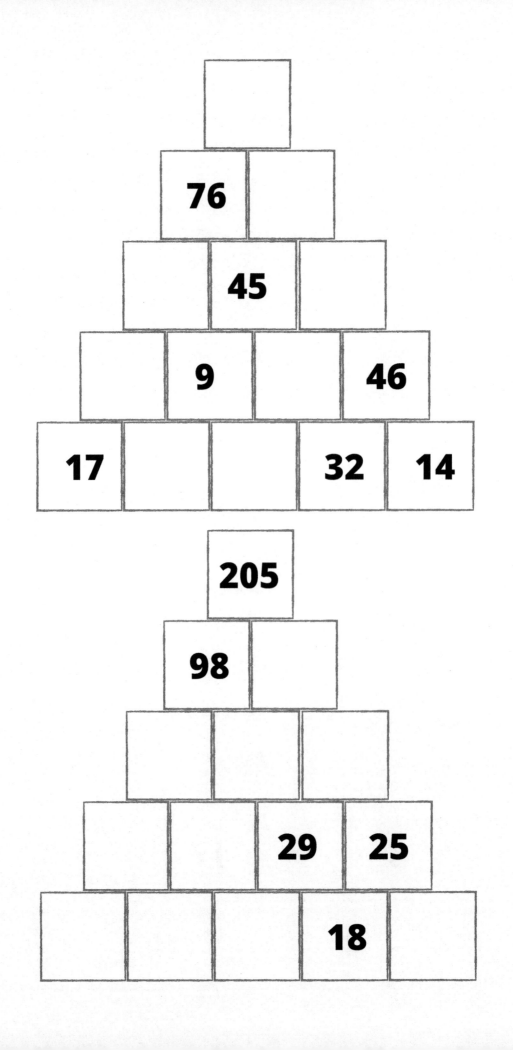

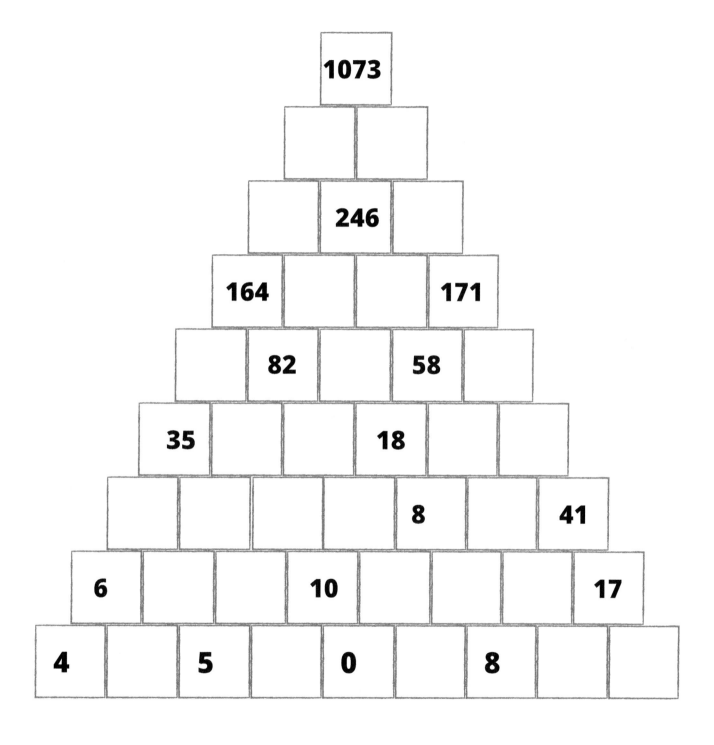

Example:

$$\begin{array}{ccc} 2 & + & 3 & = 5 \\ + & & + & \\ 4 & + & 2 & = 6 \\ = & & = & \\ 6 & & 5 & \end{array}$$

Do:

$$\begin{array}{ccc} \square & + & \square & = 9 \\ - & & - & \\ \square & - & \square & = 2 \\ = & & = & \\ 6 & & 1 & \end{array}$$

$$\begin{array}{ccc} \square & + & \square & = 12 \\ - & & + & \\ \square & - & \square & = 1 \\ = & & = & \\ 1 & & 10 & \end{array}$$

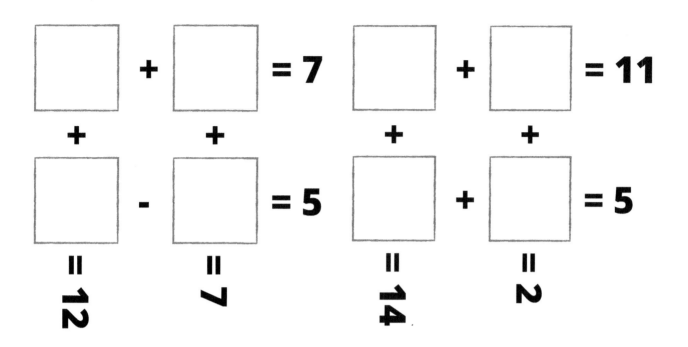

IF this: ⊞ =9   + =1

Then this: ⊢ =...

IF 2+3=10
8+4=96
7+2=63
6+5=66
THEN
9+5 = ...

IF 3, 2, 4 = 10
4, 3, 5 = 17
5, 4, 6 = 26
6, 5, 7 = 37
THEN
7, 6, 8 = ...

IF 2=6
3=12
4=20
5=30
6=42
THEN
9= ...

IF 1+4=5
2+5=12
3+6=21
THEN
8+11= ...

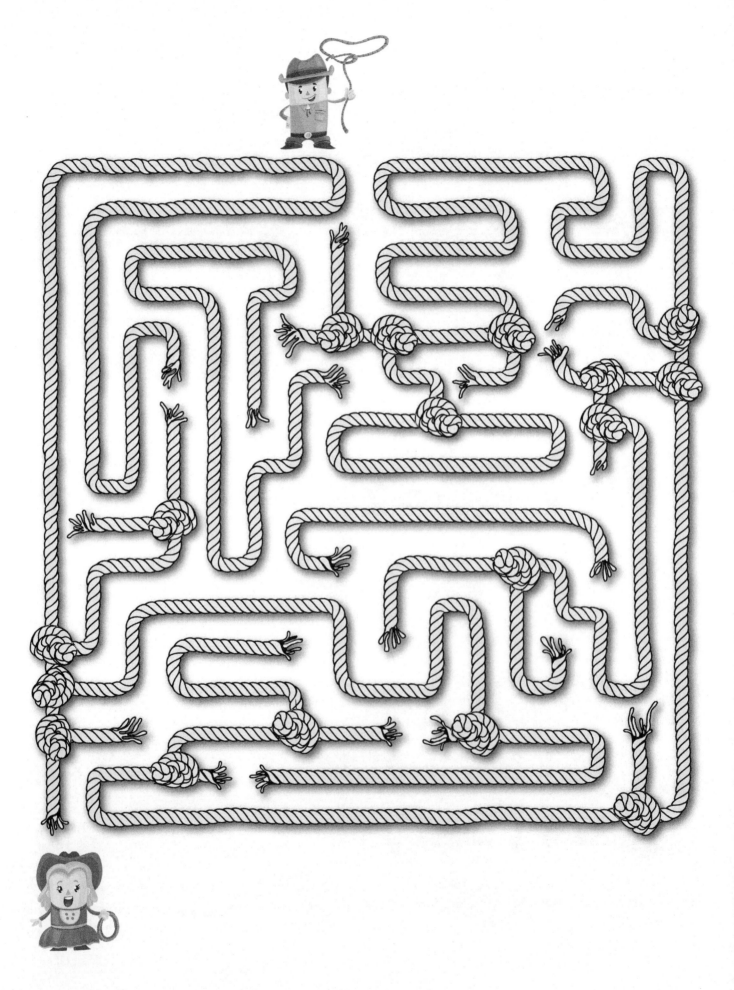

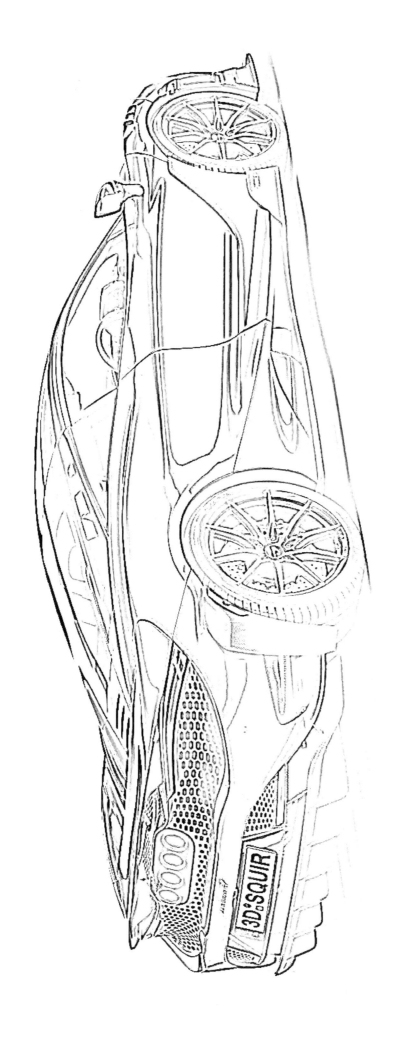

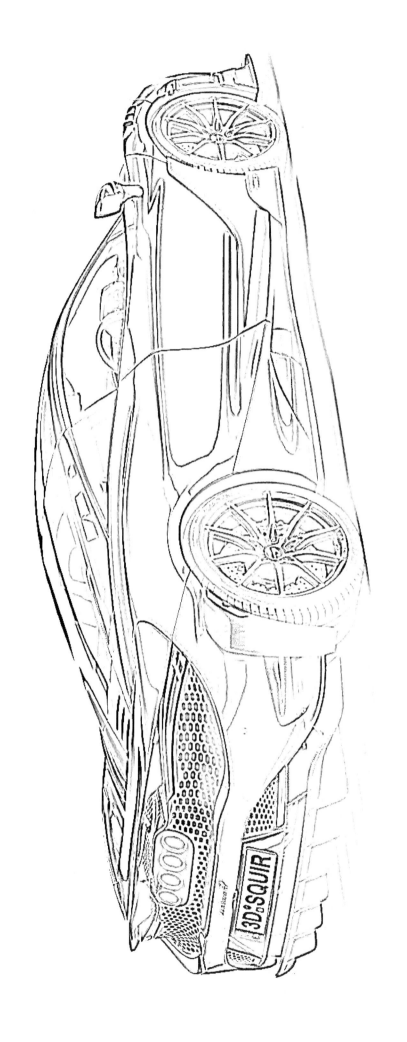

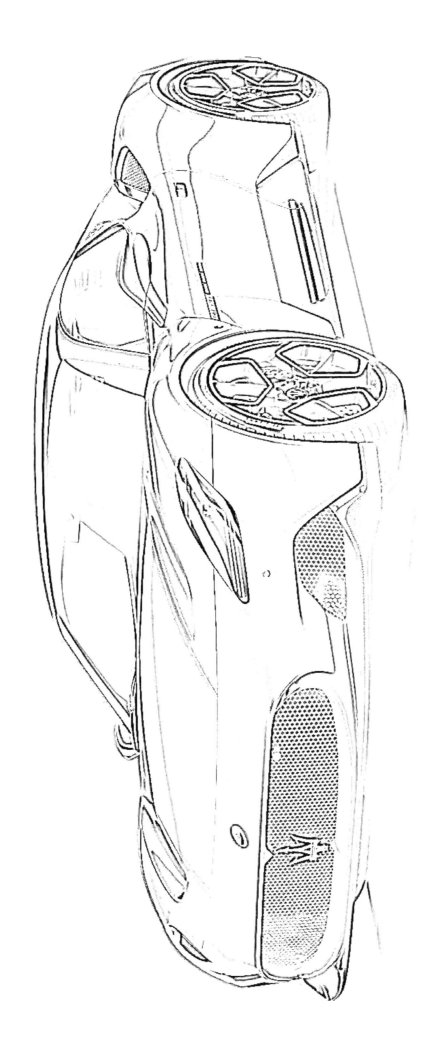

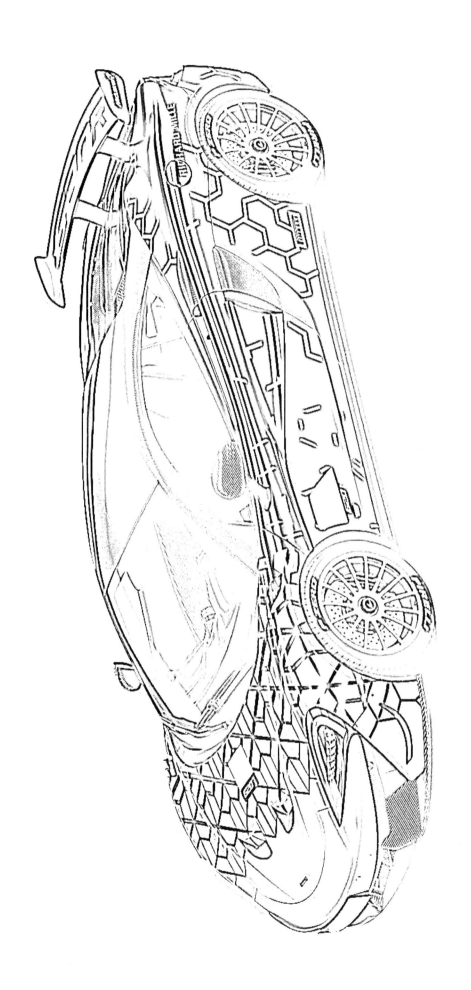

Printed in Great Britain
by Amazon